THIS FRAME ALONE

A TREATISE ON THE ILLUSION OF CONTINUITY

by

G. Om

ISBN: 979-8-9942255-0-9

This work is a contemplative exploration of experience and does not offer medical, psychological, or legal advice. Readers are encouraged to seek professional assistance where appropriate.

First paperback edition, 2025

Printed in the United States of America.

Cover design by El Mar.

DEDICATION

For the one who is ready to see.

PREFACE

There are many books that promise comfort. This is not one of them.

The view offered here questions the most fundamental assumptions human beings make about themselves and their world: that reality unfolds as a continuous stream, that events flow into one another, that a life has a shape stretching from past to future, and that a self persists unchanged beneath it all.

This book does not affirm any of those assumptions. It gently, and sometimes uncomfortably, removes them. What remains is not darkness, nor nihilism, nor despair. It is something quieter, more luminous, and far more intimate than any ideology or belief system could hope to offer. It is the seeing of reality as it unfolds, moment by moment, without the illusion of continuity imposed upon it.

Some readers may find this view strange. Others may recognize in it something familiar but never clearly perceived. A few may feel the floor drop out from beneath their habitual ways of experiencing reality.

All of these responses are welcome.

The nature of this text is not to convince, but to reveal. It does not seek followers, agreement, or adherence. It seeks only to speak clearly about what has been seen.

If something in you has been waiting—quietly, patiently—for a different way of understanding experience, then perhaps this book has something to offer. If not, nothing has been lost. Either way, you may find that the very act of reading begins to loosen the grip of the story you tell about yourself.

And perhaps, in the space that opens, something else may appear.

— G. Om

INTRODUCTION

There is a way of looking at reality that reveals its structure to be nothing like what the ordinary mind assumes. Most people perceive the world as a flowing, continuous field of experience. They imagine time unfolding like a river, each moment sliding into the next. They imagine themselves as travelers on its surface—persistent, enduring, continuous.

But the river is an illusion. There is no flow. No continuity. No traveler.

Reality arises in discrete frames—momentary appearances that vanish as soon as they are seen. What seems like continuity is merely the mind stitching together separate moments into a single narrative. This stitching is useful for survival, communication, and daily functioning. But it obscures the true nature of things.

This book is an attempt to remove the stitching.

The chapters that follow explore what remains when the illusion of continuity dissolves, and along with it the illusion of a continuous self. They examine the patterning principle known in Buddhism as karma—not as mechanistic cause and effect, but as the mysterious conditioning that gives rise to each moment's appearance. They turn toward the ethical and compassionate implications of a world without selves. And finally, they bring the reader to the threshold beyond which no treatise can speak.

This work is not meant to be believed or disbelieved. It is meant to be looked through.

If it succeeds, it may leave you not with answers, but with a different kind of seeing—a seeing that rests not on continuity, but on *this frame alone.*

◇

I

The Illusion of Continuity

The ordinary mind moves through the world as if experience were a single, unbroken stream. It assumes that life "flows," that time "passes," that events unfold in a seamless procession from before to after. This assumption is so deeply embedded that questioning it feels almost absurd—like questioning the existence of the sky or the solidity of the ground.

And yet the illusion of continuity is just that: an illusion. Its persistence does not make it real.

To see this, one must look more closely—not at the stories the mind tells, not at the interpretations layered over experience, but at experience itself, in its raw and immediate form. When awareness becomes subtle, when attention rests without grasping or naming, something unexpected becomes apparent:

Experience does not flow. It appears.

Moment by moment, frame by frame, in discrete pulses of awareness. Each one arises without reference to the one before it and vanishes without leaving a trace.

Continuity is something the mind constructs after the fact, retrofitting a narrative onto a sequence of appearances that were never causally connected. The mind imposes a sense of "before" and "after" to give coherence to what is otherwise a succession of unlinked phenomena.

Like the frames of a film, each moment of awareness is distinct. Unlike a film, there is no physical reel binding them together.

The stitching occurs solely in the mind.

This stitching is not a flaw but a function; it allows the human organism to navigate a world that seems stable and predictable. It allows memory to build an impression of a past, and imagination to build a scaffolding of a future. It allows identity to persist as a story, even though the "self" of one moment has no actual continuity with the next.

In short, continuity is a convenience—useful and adaptive, yet entirely fictional.

If one looks without conceptual overlay, the fiction dissolves. The river stops flowing. The stream becomes a single frame. Reality stands revealed as momentary.

And in that revelation, something subtle but profound occurs: The sense of "my life" begins to loosen. The sense of "myself" begins to dissolve. And suddenly the world becomes less solid, less demanding—even gossamer.

This is the first step toward seeing the true nature of reality.

To recognize the illusion of continuity is not to fall into nihilism. It is to uncover the freedom inherent in each moment—a freedom concealed by the story of a permanent self existing in a solid universe.

◇

II

DISCRETE REALITY

If continuity is an illusion, then what is real?

To speak of "discrete reality" is to point toward the structure underlying experience once conceptual stitching has been undone. It is not a doctrine or a metaphysical claim, but a direct description of how reality appears when perceived without the overlay of continuity.

In discrete reality, each moment exists by itself. Not as a slice cut from a flowing stream, but as a complete appearance— whole, self-contained, and unconnected to any moment preceding or following it.

A moment does not "come from" the previous moment. It does not "lead to" the next. It simply arises.

And then it disappears.

This arising is not caused in any conventional sense; nothing pushes the moment into existence. Nor is it random. The patterns that shape each moment are too coherent, too intricately consonant with the unfolding tapestry of lived experience to be mere chance.

The moment arises as it is because the conditions for that moment give rise to it and no other. This is the essence of karma—not as mechanical causation, but as a deep patterning of experience.

But to stay with discrete reality itself:

Look closely.

In one frame, there is the sensation of warmth. In the next, the sound of water. In the next, a thought. In the next, a shift of pressure in the body.

Each arises in isolation; the mind then stitches them into an imagined continuity.

And we say, "I felt warm water falling on my skin," as if a single subject experienced an unbroken flow of sensation. But this is not what actually occurs. What occurs is:

...a sensation...

...a sensation...

...a sensation...

each with no inherent link to any of the others.

The "link" is supplied by conceptual memory and expectation. These are not properties of the moment; they are overlays applied to it.

When the mind stops imposing continuity, each moment stands alone. And something remarkable becomes visible:

Reality is fresh.

Not metaphorically, but literally. It never repeats itself. It never persists. It never becomes anything other than what it already is.

A moment cannot hold on to itself. A sensation cannot store its own history. A thought does not generate a thinker.

This is why awakening often carries a quality of innocence. Without continuity, there is no accumulation—no burden of a past carried forward into the present. There is only the present, arising afresh, without reference to what came before.

And because each moment is unlinked, there is no self moving through time, no world persisting independently, and no continuity of identity.

There is only a flicker of existence—here and then gone.

To see this is not to withdraw from life, but to encounter it directly.

When nothing persists, nothing can be clung to. When nothing endures, nothing can be resisted.

Discrete reality is not an alternative worldview. It is the structure of experience before the mind arranges it into a story.

◇

III

KARMA AS THE PATTERNING PRINCIPLE

When continuity dissolves and experience is seen as arising in discrete frames, the question naturally emerges:

If moments do not flow from one to the next, what determines the content of each frame?

The answer is karma—though not in the simplistic, mechanistic sense often imagined. Karma is not cosmic bookkeeping. It is not reward and punishment. It is not cause and effect stretched across a linear timeline. Those notions depend on the very continuity that has already been seen as illusory.

Karma is far more subtle than that.

Karma is the patterning principle of experience: the deep, imponderable structure that gives shape to each arising moment without requiring a continuous substrate to carry it.

Each frame arises according to karmic conditions, but not because prior frames caused it in the way one billiard ball striking another causes the second ball to move. The link between moments is not causal; it is conditional. The conditions for a moment do not exist in the past—they exist in the very arising of the moment itself.

Karma is the mysterious coherence with which reality presents itself.

The Buddha listed the workings of karma among the *acinteyya*—the Imponderables—because they cannot be understood through conceptual thinking. Conceptual thinking presumes continuity. Karma functions without it.

To understand this, consider how a dream unfolds.

Dream events arise with perfect coherence—buildings, people, emotions, entire landscapes—without any physical continuity linking one moment to the next. There may be a sense of narrative, but upon waking, the dream is seen to have been constructed frame by frame, each moment complete unto itself.

The coherence of the dream did not come from continuity; it came from the mind's latent tendencies.

In waking life, the same principle applies.

Patterns of craving, fear, desire, generosity, confusion, clarity, attachment, aversion—all of these shape the arising of each moment, not as a linear chain but as a field of conditions. These conditions are not "stored" anywhere. They are not carried from one moment into the next. They appear with the moment, shaping its content, then vanish with it.

Karma is not the past acting on the present. Karma is the present arising in a patterned way.

This is why karma is incomprehensible to the ordinary mind.

The mind thinks in terms of continuity. Karma functions without continuity.

It is a principle of coherence, not causation.

Understanding karma in this way dissolves the fear that one's past is an unbreakable chain dragging behind the self. There is no self to drag, and no chain to be dragged. The patterns that appear in any moment are simply the conditions of that moment. They arise, display themselves, and vanish.

Freedom becomes possible because there is nothing to bind one moment to the next.

In each frame, mind has the opportunity to respond—or not respond—with craving or aversion. That response becomes part of the conditions shaping the next moment's appearance. But again, not as a "carryover." Rather, as an immediate unfolding of pattern.

Karma is the living tapestry of the present.

To see this clearly is to be free from fear of the past and anxiety about the future.

Indeed, the only place where suffering can arise or cease is in *this frame alone.*

◇

IV

MEMORY AND THE FICTION OF TIME

Memory seems to offer undeniable evidence that continuity exists. We remember yesterday, last year, childhood, and we take these remembered images and narratives as proof that our lives stretch backward through time in an unbroken line. The workaday mind takes memory as the anchor of identity, the guarantor of a continuous self.

But memory is not a window into the past—it is a present-moment construction.

A memory does not arise because a past moment reaches forward into the present; no past moment exists to do any reaching. Each memory appears *now*, shaped by the karmic conditions of this moment, just as every sensation, every thought, and every perception does.

The mind presents memory as if it were a retrieval—as if we dip into an archive stored somewhere inside the brain. But what appears is not the past. It is an image, a feeling, a narrative arising *now*, imbued with a flavor of the past, but devoid of any substance.

This is why, when we examine carefully, we see that memories are fluid. Memory is rewritten in the very act of remembering.

The past does not stand behind memory; memory stands alone as its own appearance.

To see memory as a present-moment construction dissolves the notion of a fixed personal history. There is no continuous thread stretching backward in time. There is only the present arising, accompanied by images and stories that appear coherent only because the mind prefers coherence over truth.

This is not to say memory is useless. It is extremely useful. Without the appearance of memory, the organism could not navigate the world. But usefulness is not existence. Memory is a functional fiction—an adaptive hallucination.

And what of the future?

The future is constructed in the same way—arising as thought, image, projection, all appearing now. The mind treats its projections as glimpses of what "will be," but they are nothing more than patterned imaginings conditioned by the present moment's tendencies.

Past and future are stories arising in the only place anything ever arises: *this frame alone.*

When memory is seen clearly, time collapses. Not because time is destroyed, but because it was never there to begin with.

What remains is the immediacy of experience, unburdened by the weight of a personal timeline. The self that depended on continuity for its existence loses its foundation. Without a continuous past, there is no continuous "me."

Only this moment remains—full, complete, and utterly unlinked from anything before or after.

V

The Myth of the Self

The illusion of continuity gives rise to many secondary illusions, but none is more persistent—or more consequential—than the illusion of a self. The self seems so obvious, so intimately known, so unquestionably real that questioning its existence seems absurd.

And yet this "self" has never been found—

not in the body

not in the mind

not in memory

not in intention

not in experience.

Every attempt to locate a self reveals only sensations, thoughts, images, impulses—each arising independently, without a single owner binding them together. The impression of ownership is fabricated in the same way continuity is fabricated: by weaving together discrete moments into a narrative that appears whole.

Any good narrative needs a protagonist. So the mind invents one—a self—which then becomes the central character in a story the mind tells to make sense of a series of unlinked frames of experience. The self is not discovered; it is imposed. And once imposed, it becomes the reference point for everything: desire, fear, identity, morality, aspiration, suffering.

But if each moment arises independently, what could persist across them to serve as a self?

The self is an inference, not an entity. A habit, not a fact. A consequence of conceptual stitching, not a feature of reality.

To see this, look closely at a moment of experience:

There is a sensation in the body. A thought arises. A feeling tones the mind. Another thought appears, followed by a shift in posture. All of it appears without a central command.

No "self" initiates these events. No "self" receives them. They simply arise.

The mind retrospectively strings them together into a story and creates a self, which then becomes an appropriator of experience: "I felt this," "I thought that," "I decided," "I acted." But these phrases describe a continuity that does not exist. For correlation is not identity, and proximity is not ownership.

The self is a grammatical convenience mistaken for a metaphysical truth.

When seen clearly, the illusion begins to dissolve. And with it, the burdens that depend on a self: the fear of annihilation, the craving for significance, the pursuit of identity, the defense of ego, the endless struggle to become someone.

What remains when the self dissolves is not nihilism but relief.

There is experience, but no owner. There is action, but no actor. There is life, but no self living it.

The disappearance of the self is not a loss. It is the lifting of a weight that was never real and never required.

What remains is freedom—quiet, spacious, and astonishingly simple.

◇

VI

THE CRAVING FOR CONTINUED EXISTENCE

Once the illusion of continuity is seen for what it is, another illusion becomes visible: the craving for continued existence. This craving is not merely the biological instinct for survival; it is far more subtle and deeply rooted. It manifests not only as the desire to remain alive, but also as the desire to remain in a particular story, as a particular someone.

To exist as a human form feels natural to those who have never experienced anything else. But for beings who have touched formless states of consciousness, or who have glimpsed modes of existence beyond embodiment, it becomes clear that human existence is simply one mode among countless others.

And yet, even the higher, more refined states of formlessness—states free from the gross suffering of embodied life—can become objects of craving.

Craving for existence is craving for location in the cosmic architecture. Craving for non-existence is craving for escape from it. Both are forms of bondage.

The Buddha described beings dwelling in luminous formless realms who remain trapped there for eons—not because they suffer, but because they cling to the bliss of those states. These realms offer no pain, no fear, no bodily limitation. They are radiant with subtle joy. But they are not liberation.

I have experienced the complete and utter nameless bliss of what some traditions call the Peak of Cyclic Existence. It is a state of unimaginable peace, infinite spaciousness, and total freedom from the burdens of form. Nothing in human experience comes close to it.

And yet—even that must be abandoned.

For as long as there is craving for existence—whether in form or in formlessness, however exalted—the wheel of becoming continues to turn. Craving for existence perpetuates the cycle; craving for non-existence also perpetuates it, because it is still craving. Only the complete cessation of craving for any type of existence or non-existence allows the illusion to fully dissolve.

This is the paradox:

The more refined and blissful a state becomes, the more seductive it is, and the more difficult it is to see through.

Human existence is coarse and filled with suffering; many yearn to escape it. Formless states are subtle and filled with delight; few yearn to escape them. And yet awakening requires releasing attachment to all states—gross or subtle, painful or blissful.

Craving for continued existence is not merely emotional. It is existential. It is the subtle movement of consciousness attempting to hold onto itself. It is the last contraction, the final veil obscuring liberation.

To see this craving clearly is to understand why various human immortality projects—religious, technological, spiritual—command such power over the mind. They promise continuity, persistence, survival. But these promises are built upon a misunderstanding of the very nature of existence.

Liberation is not the continuation of self. Liberation is the dissolution of the illusion that a self ever existed.

When craving fades, the cycle loses its momentum. When craving ends, the myth of continuity collapses. What remains is not a state—but the end of all states.

Not annihilation. Not continuation. Not becoming.

Simply an open, unconditioned, unconstructed freedom that has always been present, hidden beneath the longing to persist.

◇

VII

ETHICS WITHOUT A SELF

When the illusion of a continuous self dissolves, many people fear morality will dissolve along with it. They imagine a world without selves to be a world without responsibility, without accountability, without any coherent basis for ethical action.

But the opposite is true.

The disappearance of the self dissolves not morality, but the confusion that often masquerades as morality. What remains is a natural, effortless responsiveness—a clarity of action not rooted in obligation, reward, punishment, or identity.

Ethics without a self is not a vacuum. It is a freedom from distortion.

When there is no self to defend, there is no dishonesty. When there is no self to advance, there is no greed. When there is no self to protect, there is no hatred. When there is no self to aggrandize, there is no cruelty.

Unskillful actions do not arise because a self chooses them. They arise because confusion conditions them.

Likewise, skillful actions do not arise because a self is virtuous. They arise because clarity conditions them.

Ethics, in this view, is not a system of rules imposed upon an individual. It is the natural expression of an unconflicted mind. When craving, aversion, and delusion weaken, actions become aligned with reality rather than fantasy. Compassion flows spontaneously, not because one ought to be compassionate, but because the boundaries separating "self" from "other" have dissolved.

A self-centered morality relies on fear, guilt, pride, or tribal loyalty. It functions through narratives of identity: "I am a good person," "I must uphold my group's values," "I must conform to the expectations of my community."

But when the self is revealed to be fictional, these motivations lose their foundation. What remains is a morality grounded not in identity but in direct perception.

Seeing clearly, one acts clearly.

In this clarity, harmful actions lose their appeal. They no longer serve any imagined purpose, no longer reinforce any imagined self, no longer provide the gratification of egoic victory or the anesthetic of egoic distraction.

What is left is a kind of ethical simplicity:

If an action reduces suffering, it is skillful. If an action increases suffering, it is unskillful.

This simplicity is not naive. It is precise. It recognizes that suffering arises from confusion—the belief in a self that must be defended, enhanced, secured, and perpetuated. When that confusion dissolves, the actions that once flowed from it dissolve as well.

Ethics without a self is not a philosophical position. It is the lived expression of awakening.

It arises on its own, the way light fills a room when a window is opened. Nothing is added; an obstruction is removed.

In the space left open by the absence of self, compassion becomes the only coherent response to the world.

◇

VIII

COMPASSION AS THE ONLY COHERENT RESPONSE

When the illusions of continuity and self dissolve, the world does not become cold or indifferent. It becomes almost unbearably *intimate*. Without the barrier of a self to defend, and without the narrative of a life to uphold, every moment of experience appears in its raw, unfiltered presence.

Nothing is "mine." Nothing is "other." Everything simply *is*.

In this immediacy, compassion is not a virtue to be cultivated. It is not a moral project, a religious duty, or an ethical achievement. Compassion is what naturally arises when the boundaries that separate beings are seen to be imaginary.

Suffering is recognized not as "their suffering," but simply as suffering. Joy is recognized not as "their joy," but simply as joy. Experience is recognized not as "my experience" or "your experience," but simply as experience.

This recognition transforms the relationship between awareness and the world. The distance collapses. The imagined separation between subject and object dissolves. What appears is a seamless field in which the well-being of one part is inseparable from the well-being of the whole.

Compassion is the only coherent response because anything else would require the reconstitution of the illusion of self.

21

Cruelty requires a self. Hatred requires a self. Indifference requires a self. Greed requires a self.

When the self falls away, none of these can be sustained. They become impossible, not because one suppresses them, but because they have no foothold in a mind that sees clearly.

This compassion is not sentimental. It is not emotional excess or empathic overwhelm. It is not pity, which presumes a hierarchy between helper and helped.

True compassion is the effortless expression of non-separation.

It is gentle because gentleness harms nothing. It is patient because there is no self whose urgency must be satisfied. It is generous because nothing is mine to withhold. It is fearless because there is no self to protect.

In this sense, compassion is not an activity but an orientation—a way the world expresses itself when seen without distortion. It is not something one *does*, but rather something one becomes transparent to.

When compassion flows in this way, it requires no justification. It needs no reward, no recognition, no story.

It simply arises, the way a flower opens in sunlight.

And just as effortlessly, it passes away—leaving no residue, no expectation, no identity built around being compassionate.

Compassion is the natural fragrance of awakening.

When the illusions of continuity and self dissolve, what remains is this:

an open, boundless field of awareness in which everything that appears is met with the same quiet, unconditional care.

◇

IX

THE WAY BEYOND THIS TREATISE

Every concept in this book has been offered as a pointer, not a description. The deepest truths cannot be captured in language because language depends on distinction, separation, and continuity—the very illusions this text attempts to illuminate.

A finger pointing toward the moon is not the moon. A map is not the territory. A teaching is not the truth.

The purpose of this treatise is not to construct a new philosophical system. It is to undo the systems that obscure direct perception. Nothing written here is meant to be believed. Belief belongs to the realm of thought, and thought belongs to the realm of conceptual continuity.

Awakening is not conceptual.

It is the recognition that reality does not need a story to be what it is. Nothing is gained by seeing this. Nothing is lost. The world continues to appear—sounds, sensations, emotions, thoughts—but without the insistence on a someone to whom they belong.

The illusion collapses. This frame alone remains.

When seen clearly, the compulsive need to make sense of everything relaxes. Experience no longer demands interpretation. Life is no longer framed as a narrative arc. The mind becomes quiet not through suppression, but because its foundational assumptions have been seen through.

The dissolution of illusion is not an attainment. It is a release.

What remains is simple, direct, unconstructed. It cannot be owned or improved, pursued or attained. It is not a final state. It is not an achievement. It is not even an understanding.

It is the transparency of awareness to itself.

From here, nothing needs to be added. The treatise has reached the limit of what can be written or spoken. Beyond this point, words collapse under their own weight.

What lies beyond is not mysterious. It is simply unspeakable.

The way beyond this treatise is the way beyond every conceptual framework. There is nothing to adopt, nothing to reject, nothing to hold. Life continues to unfold exactly as before—appearance after appearance, frame after frame—but the illusion of continuity no longer binds it together.

Reality stands free, and so do you.

Not because you have become free, but because the one who sought freedom was never there.

◇◇◇

AFTERWORD

There is a moment in every sincere inquiry when language has done all it can do. Not because truth has been reached, but because truth was never something that language could touch.

Concepts can gesture. Metaphors can illuminate. Reasoning can untangle knots of confusion.

But none of these can reveal what is already present.

Every word in this book has been a raft—a temporary structure meant to carry the mind across the current of its own assumptions. When the far shore is reached, the raft may be safely discarded. And when it is seen that the river itself was only ever a construct of the mind, even the idea of a crossing dissolves.

There is no continuity to uphold. No self to defend. No final understanding to achieve.

There is only this: reality revealed in its immediacy, free from the interpretations that once obscured it.

If something in these pages has loosened the grip of the narratives you once believed—if it has created even a slight opening through which the present moment may be seen more clearly—then the text has served its purpose.

What remains is the simplicity of experience appearing as *this frame alone.*

ABOUT THE AUTHOR

G. Om writes from direct contemplative insight rather than philosophical speculation.

He offers no doctrine and claims no authority.